Millicent Has A Party

Janet Noonan and Jacqueline Calvert
Illustrated by Bartholomew

Chariot Books™
David C. Cook Publishing Co.

Chariot Books™ is an imprint of David C. Cook Publishing Co.

David C. Cook Publishing Co., Elgin, Illinois 60120
David C. Cook Publishing Co., Weston, Ontario

MILLICENT HAS A PARTY

Illustrated by Bartholomew

Book and cover design by Catherine Colten

First Printing, 1990
Printed in Singapore
94 93 92 91 90 5 4 3 2 1

Library of Congress Cataloging-in-Publication Data
Noonan, Janet
Millicent has a party/Janet Noonan and Jacquelyn Calvert; illustrated by Bartholomew.
p.cm.—(Mind your manners, please)
Summary: Rhymed text and illustrations describe what happens when Millicent behaves badly at her own party and how much more pleasant it is for everyone when she remembers her manners.
1. Etiquette for children and youth. 2. Entertaining—Juvenile literature. 3. Children's parties—Juvenile literature. [1. Etiquette. 2. Behavior. 3. Parties. 4. Christian life.] I. Calvert, Jacquelyn. II. Bartholomew, ill. III. Title. IV. Series: Noonan, Janet, Mind your manners, please.
BJ1857.C5N66 1989 88-38783
395'.3—dc 19 CIP
ISBN 1-55513-983-3 AC

When Millicent Forgets Her

Manners

Millicent has a party,
And when the children come
She hides behind the door.
Why does she act so dumb?

HAP

Millicent has a party.
When Todd hands her a gift,
She rips apart the package—
Then throws it at him, miffed.

Millicent has a party,
But when the guests begin to play
With all her pretty presents
She snatches them away.

Millicent has a party.
They play musical chairs.
She naughtily breaks the rules
And says, "Oh, well, who cares?"

Millicent has a party.
And grabs the wildest hat.
She yells, “I want to wear it.
“It’s my birthday, and that’s that.”

Millicent has a party.
Mom serves praline ice cream.
"I want vanilla," she pouts
And then begins to scream.

Millicent has a party
And, asked to cut the cake,
She slips off all the roses,
Then puts them on her plate.

Millicent has a party.
When her guests say good-bye,
She shouts, "If you go home now
"I will just have to cry."

Dear God,
When Mom gives me a party
Please help me be polite,
Be gracious to my friends,
And treat them all just right.

When Millicent Minds Her Manners

Millicent has a party,
And when the doorbell rings,
Invites the guests to enter,
Then smiles and takes their things.

Millicent has a party.
She's given gifts with bows—
Opens each one gently—
Admires with "ahs" and "ohs."

Millicent has a party,
And asks her friends to play
With all her prettiest gifts
As long as they can stay.

HAPPY

Millicent has a party.
They play her favorite game.
She politely minds the rules
And others do the same.

Millicent has a party.
When served praline ice cream
She quietly says, "Thank you."
She likes it, it would seem.

Millicent has a party
And asked to cut the cake,
She puts a yummy rose
On everybody's plate.

Millicent has a party,
And when her guests must go
Says, "Thank you all for coming.
I did enjoy it so."

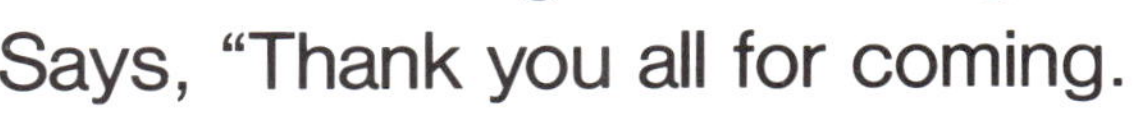

Dear God,
Parties are special
Since You've taught me the way
To behave when playmates come
To celebrate my day.